MW01106434

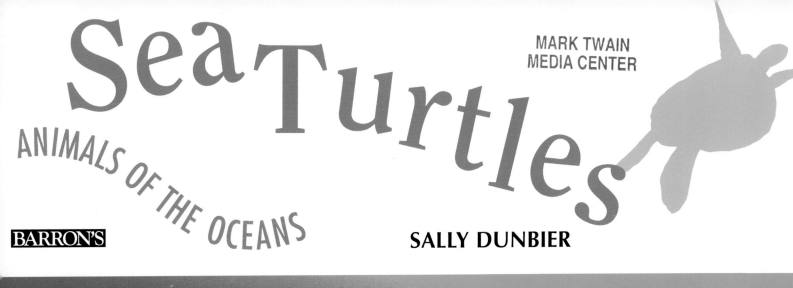

Sea Turtles

ANIMALS OF THE OCEANS

MARK TWAIN
MEDIA CENTER

BARRON'S

SALLY DUNBIER

CONTENTS

INTRODUCTION

With their strange leathery flippers and beautifully patterned hard shells, sea turtles are ancient-looking ocean creatures. Their ancestors walked the earth 200 million years ago and were very much bigger than today. The first turtles were massive animals with large clawed feet, 10- to 23- feet long shells and weighing up to three tons. That's bigger than a medium-sized car!

Turtles are classed as reptiles. This means they are omniviparous (they lay their eggs on land), breathe through lungs, are cold-blooded (body temperature changes with their surroundings), and have scaly skin. Other reptiles include crocodiles, snakes, and lizards. Apart from sea snakes, sea turtles are the only reptiles who live mainly in the ocean.

Because sea turtles are found in the depths of the sea and come ashore briefly in isolated places, it was difficult to learn a lot about them. But with the developments in underwater diving equipment and new tracking methods,

scientists in recent times have discovered much more.

We now know that there are seven species of sea turtle ranging from the largest – the leatherback, weighing in at up to 660 pounds – to the smallest, called the Kemp's ridley, which reaches around 90 pounds.

Sea turtles are found in almost all of the world's oceans, usually in the warmer regions. Some species travel huge distances in yearly journeys between their feeding and breeding grounds. And they are all endangered species – mainly due to the impact of humans.

Left: First march toward the sea: a newborn sea turtle hatchling makes its first dangerous journey across the beach.

A relative of the dinosaur, the mighty sea turtle emerges from the ocean.

DIFFERENT KINDS OF TURTLES

As it scours the coral reef, a hawksbill displays the distinctive designs for which it is known on its skin, foreflippers, and head.

The seven species of sea turtles are divided into two groups. One family covers six species, all of which have hard shells made up of scutes (round plates). The other category relates only to the leatherback, with its thick skin-covered shell divided by ridges.

Sea turtles can sometimes be confused with freshwater turtles and tortoises. Their freshwater cousins found in lakes, ponds, and estuaries have long necks and can pull their neck, tail, and legs into their shells. They are classed as terrapins. Other relatives, the tortoises, live completely on land and have leg-like limbs and toed feet.

Unlike tortoises, sea turtles only come on land to nest or, in a few cases, to sunbathe. And in contrast to freshwater turtles, sea

turtles have thick necks and flipper-like legs, which are not able to be pulled back into their shells.

The turtle's shell is divided into two sections – the rounded top layer, called the carapace, and the flatter underpart known as the plastron. Scientists have used this unique shell as one of the main ways of grouping sea turtle species. Both the scute designs on the shell and the patterns on the skin are very distinctive. Through the plastron's shape, size, color, and texture, we can recognize different types of turtles. The shell is also used to estimate the turtle's size. A sea turtle's length is measured from the tip of its shell to the tail.

With its ridged, skin-covered shell and impressive size, the leatherback is a striking sight.

Beautifully patterned shells and intricately lined skin are two features that identify a green turtle.

AUSTRALIAN FLATBACKS

Australian flatbacks are named for their distinctive flattish carapaces. Unlike all other sea turtles, flatbacks prefer to stay in one region, the warm shallow waters of Australia's northern coast.

Flatbacks are often called the most primitive sea turtles. They are medium-sized, growing to between 2½ and 3 feet in length, and have a gray shell with creamy gray legs and tail. Flatbacks scour the seabed and surface area to dine on a number of Australian delicacies – sea cucumbers, prawns, mollusks and jellyfish – that are found not too far from the shore.

Females make their nests on top of sand dunes, laying a clutch (group) of about 55 eggs. This is much less than other sea turtles, but the hatchlings (baby turtles), at slightly more than 2 inches long, are bigger than their cousins. Young flatbacks are more likely to survive than other species as they can fight off some of their smaller enemies, are strong swimmers, and stay in shallower waters.

Although their front and back flippers are designed for sea travel, the flatback manages the journey over the sand surprisingly quickly.

KEMP'S RIDLEYS

The Kemp's ridley is the world's smallest sea turtle at about 28 inches in length. Emerging from their eggs at less than 2 inches in length, hatchlings are dark gray in color. As they grow into adults the coloring changes to an olive green carapace with a yellowish plastron. Shells are somewhat heart shaped.

Scientists only classed Kemp's ridleys as a separate species in 1963 after making a fascinating discovery. It was not known where the turtles nested until an old 1947 film was unearthed that showed about 40,000 Kemp's ridleys nesting on a strip of Mexican beach: Rancho Nuevo. Unlike most other sea turtles, Kemp's ridleys take part in a mass nesting each year between April and August – always returning to exactly the same beach. The group egg layings are called arribabas, Spanish for "arrival." Just 500 Kemp's ridleys came to nest at Rancho Nuevo in 1992.

Today the turtles are found mostly in the Gulf of Mexico, where they feed on crabs, shellfish, and snails.

The Kemp's ridley sea turtle is not only the world's smallest sea turtle, it is also the most endangered.

GREEN TURTLES

Green turtles are so called not for their outer coloring but because of their greenish body fat. For hundreds of years their meat has been used to make green turtle soup – a sought-after specialty food.

The green turtle can grow up to 3 feet long – and has a heart-shaped shell. Body color can range from olive brown to gray or black with spots. One of its main features is its beak, which has a saw-like lower part. This part is used to rip up sea grass – the green turtle's

Preparing for the nesting season on Isabella Island, Galapagos, a group of female green turtles bask at the water's surface and on the beach.

main food as an adult. Unusually, when the green turtle is young it is a carnivore (meat eater) and becomes a vegetarian (plant eater) only later in life.

The largest number of green turtles is found in the waters off Australia. They are also found

The green turtle's scissor-sharp beak is designed for grazing on sea vegetation such as algae.

around Central and South America, Florida, the Philippines, and the Pacific Islands. These turtles are great travelers, swimming up to 1500 miles from their feeding grounds to nesting beaches. The trip the turtles make from coastal Brazil to Ascension Island, off the coast of Africa, is an example of one of their vast sea journeys.

Green turtles are keen sunbathers and can sometimes be found basking among seaweed on the ocean's surface or lying on a secluded beach. They are also known to have underwater sleeping shelters to which they return each evening.

A green turtle coasts over a coral reef in Hawaii.

HAWKSBILLS

The medium-sized hawksbill can grow to about 3 feet in length and up to 135 pounds in weight. It has a bird-like head and beak, but is probably most famous for its beautiful shell. Tortoiseshell – highly prized for centuries for hairpins, ornaments, and wall hangings – comes not from the land tortoise, but from the sea-dwelling hawksbill turtle. The scutes of the turtle's shell overlap into an ornate pattern forming a shield shape in a striking marbled golden/brown color.

The adult hawksbill, found in waters off Florida, the Bahamas, and in the Gulf of Mexico, has a narrow diet made up almost entirely of sea sponges. Scientists have yet to discover how hawksbills can eat these sponges without any ill effects, as they are poisonous. When they are

Sea turtles hold a strong fascination for people. Here a hawksbill is unconcerned about meeting a diver.

Viewed from below, a hawksbill hatchling takes its first plunge into the sea.

young, hawksbills feed along coral reefs close to the water's surface, only managing to make the deep dives for sponges when they get older.

Hawksbill nests are built in isolated areas, high up on the beach among roots and plants. Females often spread nests out along the beach in order to make it more difficult for predators, such as birds, land animals, and people, who raid their egg clutches.

Left: Displaying the beautiful shield-shaped shell for which it is famous, a hawksbill glides over the seabed in Japan.

LEATHERBACKS

The leatherback turtle stands out from other sea turtles with its leathery, ridged shell and powerful forelimbs. Blackish in color with white spots, the leatherback's long oval-shaped shell is made up of skin-covered bony plates instead of the scutes other sea turtle species have. All leatherbacks have seven ridges running down their backs.

The leatherback is the king of sea turtles – it's the biggest, the deepest diver, the best swimmer, and the greatest traveler. The largest one ever recorded was 10 feet in length, and they can reach weights of up to 800 pounds – about the size of a large hot tub!

Leatherbacks also differ from other sea turtles in the way they can cope with colder temperatures. This species is able to control its own body temperature so that it can dive down to huge depths (more than half a mile). Near the sea

You can see the sheer size and bulk of the leatherback when viewed next to a person.

Opposite: This female leatherback has come ashore to nest. Because their eyes are accustomed to sea water, they weep tears when they come ashore.

bottom, where leatherbacks catch their food, temperatures can fall to as low as 6°C (43°F).

Found in all the world's oceans, from as far south as southern Chile to as far north as Canada, leatherbacks are known to cover huge distances – up to 3000 miles. Traveling in groups, the turtles follow the same routes in their underwater journeys every year, often along deep-sea corridors. Their huge front flippers make them strong swimmers and help them snare jellyfish, their favorite food.

Leatherbacks nest together in groups, and the females often fool enemies by creating false nests. Another trick is the way in which they can lay yolkless (infertile) eggs. Some scientists think that, because these eggs are found at the top of the nest, they are laid to protect the "real" eggs below.

Huge, ancient-looking fore-flippers pull the leatherback through the water at surprisingly fast speeds.

LOGGERHEADS

As you might guess by its name, the loggerhead can be recognized by its very large, thickset head. With widths of up to 10 inches, this turtle's head often looks oversized for the rest of its body. Reddish-brown in color with yellow segments, the loggerhead has a distinctive shell that thickens out at the end. This large turtle can grow up to 40 inches in length and weigh up to 350 pounds.

The loggerhead is widespread throughout the world's oceans, but although it travels long distances – and has been found more than 500 miles from shore – it is quite a slow swimmer.

With its wide, strong jaws, the loggerhead enjoys many different foods – seaweed and marine grasses, as well as fish, jellyfish, shellfish, squid, and shrimp. They are known to group together in large colonies for "banquets" at certain times of the year. The Baja California coast is a favorite spot for mass feedings. When the area's red crabs are numerous, about

Displaying its oversized head, a loggerhead swims with a diver.

10,000 young loggerheads have been recorded flocking together to feed on them.

Female loggerheads come ashore to lay their eggs in many different locations. Nesting grounds are found on Masirah Island in Oman and on the islands off the southeastern United States.

Above: New to the world, a loggerhead breaks out of its egg.

Seemingly unfazed by being caught on film and having a fish hitching a ride, a large loggerhead glides through the sea.

OLIVE RIDLEYS

The shell of the olive ridley is murky-colored and has large scutes with fluted edges.

Like Kemp's ridleys, olive ridleys are among the smallest sea turtles, growing up to 2½ feet long and weighing up to 90 pounds. They are also the most common sea turtles.

With heart shaped shells – olive green above and yellowish on the undersides – olive ridleys travel throughout the world's tropical waters. They are a very frequent bycatch of the hauls brought in by shrimp trawlers. Each year many thousands are recorded in shrimp nets in coastal South America.

Olive ridleys win the prize for being the "Most Speedy Nesters." They take only 45 minutes (compared to several hours with other

species) to come ashore, make a nest, lay eggs, and return to the water. Again, like Kemp's ridleys, they nest together in large groups that are also called arribabas. But instead of picking one beach, the olive ridleys are found in many locations. The mouths of rivers and estuaries in Mexico, India, Costa Rica, and Nicaragua are favorite nesting grounds. Olive ridleys can nest

After making the nesting chamber, this female olive ridley goes into a trance as she lays the eggs.

throughout the year instead of during particular seasons as other turtles do. Nesting times are often chosen according to ocean tide patterns.

Fond of crabs, shrimp, and jellyfish, this small, versatile sea turtle is another long-distance traveler. One was once found 1500 miles from where it had been nesting – that's about the driving distance between New York City and Dallas, Texas!

With its protruding upper jaw and oval face, the olive ridley's head is very bird-like.

Sea turtles are relatives of prehistoric reptiles, as can be seen by looking at their leathery, lined skin and peculiar domed shell.

THE SEA TURTLE'S BODY

The sea turtle's main distinctive feature is its shell, which is made up of fused bone. The turtle's rib cage and spine are connected to the inside of the upper shell – the carapace. On the outer part of the carapace is a fibrous layer called keratin, which gives the shell its color.

For all turtles except leatherbacks, interlocking plates known as "scutes" join to form the shell. The underlayer of shell, the plastron, is usually a lighter color. The carapace and plastron are joined at the sides by bridges of fused bone covering a thick layer of skin.

Sea turtles lack teeth. Their jaws are similar to beaks, often with scissor-sharp edges.

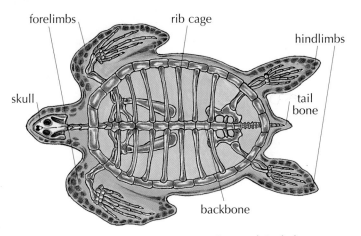

forelimbs rib cage hindlimbs

skull

tail bone

backbone

Sea turtle's skeleton

The green turtle's flat, pale-colored plastron contrasts with the rounded, dark shell above.

The limbs are rather like paddles, and the forelimbs are much larger and stronger than those at the rear. All sea turtles have a small tail at the end of their shell – in most cases, the tails of full-grown males are longer than those of females.

Covering the head, neck, limbs, and tail is the distinctive scaly skin that is common to all reptiles. This tough, thick layer protects the turtle from attack and injury. It also retains a lot of moisture.

To survive in saltwater, sea turtles have an unusual way of removing the salt from their systems – through tear ducts. They are able to take in seawater and then get rid of the salt through small glands by the eyes. By changing marine water into fresh water, turtles can prevent dehydration.

SENSES, BREATHING, AND MOVING

Sea turtles have to breathe air to survive, but they don't need nearly as much oxygen as humans. The amount of time they spend underwater depends on how active they are. If they are making deep dives, they come to the surface about every four minutes; but they can sleep on the seafloor for several hours without moving. Some species of turtle are known to hibernate completely by burrowing into the sand when sea temperatures reach very low levels.

Sea turtles' senses are specially developed for underwater life – their sense of smell is strong and their vision is good in the water, but weak on land. They have no external ear holes, but their inner ears pick up a reasonable amount of sound in the sea.

The sea turtle is graceful in the water. Some species reach surprisingly high swimming speeds – up to 15 miles per hour.

In motion, many sea turtles, such as the green turtle, flap their large forelimbs up and down like birds' wings. The smaller hind flippers are flattened out at the back and help with turning. Between flapping movements that build up speed, the turtles coast swiftly through the water.

A green sea turtle gracefully cruises above rippled sand off the coast of Western Australia. The bones in a sea turtle's foreflippers are flattened out especially for sea travel.

Sea turtle's internal organs

Blood vessels

Lungs

Heart

Small intestine

Trachea

Cloaca

Liver

Bladder

Far more at home in the water, the adult sea turtle's progress on land is painfully slow.

Although they lack external ears, sea turtles have inner ear drums that enable them to hear reasonably well.

LIFE CYCLE

Sea turtles can live for quite a long time – at least 30 years, and some for as long as 70 years.

Sea turtles do not have partners and there is no courtship stage before mating. When a female turtle is ready to breed, several males will compete to mate with her, and they will often attack the male who succeeds. Once mating has taken place, the fertilized eggs take 30 days to develop.

Egg laying usually occurs twice during the female's breeding season. Nesting beaches are generally isolated and provide an easy route to

Above: Having escaped from the hazards on the shore, hatchlings head for the ocean. Only a very few will survive the perils there.

the waterline for the young hatchlings once they emerge from the eggs.

The nests are almost always made on the higher level of the shore at night, for safety reasons. The female ambles clumsily ashore, makes her way up the beach, and digs a hole (called the nesting chamber) in the sand with her hind flippers. She goes into a kind of trance for 1–2 hours and lays 80–120 eggs. The turtle then covers the nest carefully with sand and makes the slow trip back to the water. She will have nothing more to do with her offspring.

Two months later the hatchlings break out of their eggs. They instinctively know that they must start their journey across the sand to the sea. On the way they are exposed to many enemies: crabs, land animals, birds, and people on the beach, and various sea dwellers in the water. Hatchlings have a very low rate of survival – only about one in every 1000 will make it to adulthood.

The young sea turtles are able to swim as soon as they enter the water. Those that become full grown will join others in extraordinary underwater journeys.

Above: Flicking back sand energetically with her hind flippers, this sea turtle is making a nest in the sand.

A female loggerhead lays her eggs in the nesting chamber. She will produce about 80–120 eggs the size of golf balls.

23

TURTLES IN HISTORY

Sea turtles are featured in the folklore of many cultures throughout the world. In one ancient Chinese myth, the world is described as a gigantic turtle. The underpart of the shell, the plastron, represents the world's oceans and land surface. The carapace is the sky and heavens, containing the sun, moon, stars, and planets.

In the United States, many Native American tribes believed that the land on which they lived was the shell of a mother turtle, floating in a massive sea. And in Hawaii a number of traditional tales describe how sea turtles help in battles and transport gods and chiefs on their backs.

Turtle products, such as tortoiseshell and turtle meat, have also been highly prized by many peoples over the centuries.

Green turtle soup was a sought-after delicacy that has been around for hundreds of years. People throughout Europe and Asia would go to great lengths to sample it. In 18th-century England another dish called mock turtle soup was devised. This used calves' heads or cows' tails instead of turtle because green turtle meat was too expensive.

John Tenniel's illustration of the Mock Turtle from Lewis Carroll's book, *Alice in Wonderland*.

24

Left: This unique tortoiseshell mask dates back to 1870. Made by a Torres Strait Islander, it depicts a face with a European-style hat.

An ancient Mexican figurine dating from the Columbian period (the 7th to the 10th century) shows a sea turtle body with a human head.

Today green turtles have become an endangered species, and trading in any turtle meat is strictly banned in most countries.

It is also now illegal to use tortoiseshell – which comes from the exquisite shell of the hawksbill turtle – throughout most of the world. But it was once widely used and valued. In China during the Shang Dynasty (1766–1122 B.C.), whole hawksbill shells were used in fortune-telling ceremonies. And in Japan, until quite recently, tortoiseshell was used in the ancient tradition of carving ceremonial bridal combs.

SEA TURTLES AND PEOPLE

Life is difficult for baby and juvenile sea turtles, but once they have matured they should be equipped to survive easily. However, this is not the case for one major reason: people.

In many parts of the world, turtle eggs, stolen from nests by poachers, are still sought after and sold in local markets. Shrimp fishing – particularly off the coasts of Florida and South America – kills thousands of sea turtles every year when they get caught up with the shrimp in huge fishing nets.

The sea turtle egg-laying process is intriguing for people, and at some nesting sites, such as Terengganu in Malaysia, large groups of people crowd around the sea turtle on her nest. This creates an unsuitable atmosphere for the shy creatures. In other places, such as Florida,

A poacher examines the sea turtle eggs he has collected. Trade in eggs is banned in most countries.

Turtle watching is a popular activity, but artificial light and touching the turtle is disturbing for the creature.

Right: Commercial fishing has devastated sea turtle populations. Here, a sea turtle has been caught on a Spanish fishing line in the Mediterranean.

seaside housing areas have been built very close to turtle nesting beaches. Human-made structures such as sea walls, built to stop erosion, and introduced plants have altered these beaches' natural formation, making them unsuitable for turtle nesting.

The remnants from today's human communities on land have also invaded the sea turtles' watery home. Chemicals and human waste have made parts of the ocean too toxic for turtles to survive. When there is an oil spill, for instance, the poisonous chemicals get into the sea turtle's system when it comes to the surface to breathe. Large numbers of sea turtles swallow plastic bags, mistaking them for jellyfish, which kill them. Leatherbacks, in particular, are caught on oceanic longlines.

THE FUTURE FOR SEA TURTLES

All species of sea turtle now face the danger of becoming extinct. Leatherback numbers have dwindled down to just one third of the total population in 1980. They are no longer found at all in the western

Pacific Ocean. And there are now probably less than 1000 Kemp's ridleys alive.

Fortunately, there are many scientists, conservationists, and turtle lovers who are dedicated to saving sea turtles. They are actively working to protect sea turtle nests, hatchlings, adults, and environments to ensure that all species survive the 21st century.

Several international agreements banning all imports and exports of turtle products are now in place. The CITES (Convention on International Trade in Endangered Fauna and Flora) treaty, signed by 120 countries, protects all sea turtles from trading activity. An attempt by Cuba and Japan to allow the resumption of trade in hawksbill shells was defeated at the CITES 2000 meeting. And the Convention on Migratory Species of Wild Animals has set out conservation guidelines for all countries to follow.

The Center for Marine Conservation, based in Washington, D.C., supports sea turtle projects worldwide. The group was involved in making turtle excluder devices (TEDs) compulsory on

Opposite: On an unspoiled beach on Bartolome Island, Galapagos, a female green turtle returns to the sea after nesting.

Above: A scientist monitors a sea turtle laying eggs at Turtle Island Park, Malaysia.

Left: Students in Punaluu Bay, Hawaii, examine a green turtle. They are collecting important information to help sea turtles.

Sea turtle hatchlings at Heron Island, Australia, are collected to be moved to a refuge.

all shrimp boats in the United States and many other countries. TEDs are like trapdoors in the shrimp nets: special areas through which the turtles can escape. The Sea Turtle Survival League is part of the earliest marine turtle organization, the Caribbean Conservation Corp. (CCC). Members organize many sea turtle research and education activities, including a turtle adoption project.

In many areas scientists and local people are working together to help sea turtles. The Earthwatch Institute sea turtle project is based at a major leatherback nesting site – Playa Granda in Costa Rica. The Institute helped set up a national park, worked with locals to stop turtle egg poaching and net fishing, and today closely monitors all turtles who come ashore to nest. Sea turtle lovers are invited to become Earthwatch volunteers and join the project at Playa Granda to help with turtle research.

In recent years many countries have set aside sea turtle havens and refuges. On the east coast of Florida, the Archie Carr Wildlife Refuge has bought a 20-mile stretch of beach to safeguard the nesting sites (the biggest in the United States) of loggerheads and green turtles. Another major loggerhead nesting beach in Dalyan, Turkey, is now protected. And on the island of Zakynthos in Greece a special nature reserve for nesting loggerheads has been created.

In 1999, responding to the huge number of leatherbacks being hooked by swordfish fishers a protected zone was set up in the Pacific Ocean north of Hawaii. All longline fishing is now banned for two years throughout a huge area measuring 1000 miles in width.

Many sea turtle hatcheries have been set up at important nesting sites in countries such as Costa Rica, Mexico, and Malaysia. Eggs are collected from the nests and moved to a safe enclosure for hatching. The hatchlings are later released into the water once they have grown enough to have a better chance of survival. In some cases, to help stop egg poaching, local villagers are given a small percentage of the turtle eggs to sell legally.

People throughout the world are now learning more about the plight of the sea turtle. Hopefully, efforts will be made to ensure that these magnificent creatures will still be around for everyone to enjoy for many years to come.

In order for sea turtles to survive, their beautiful marine home has to remain unpolluted.

INDEX

First published in 2000 by David Bateman Ltd,
30 Tarndale Grove, Albany Business Park,
Albany, Auckland, New Zealand

Copyright © David Bateman Ltd, 2000

First edition for the United States and Canada
published by Barron's Educational Series, Inc., 2000

All rights reserved.

No part of this book may be reproduced in any form,
by photostat, microfilm, xerography, or any other means, or
incorporated into any information retrieval system, electronic or
mechanical, without the written permission of the copyright
owner.

Text: Sally Dunbier, B.A.
Photographs: New Zealand Picture Library except for Andy
Belcher p. 1, p. 21 (bottom); ANT Photolibrary p. 6; Sarah
Irvine, Florida Marine Research Institute p. 7; Photobank p. 4,
p. 10, p.11, p. 12 (left), p. 17 (bottom), p. 20; Tui De Roy p. 8,
p. 16, p. 18, p. 28; Superstock Photo Library p. 25 (right);
Te Papa Tongarewa/Museum of New Zealand p. 25 (left);
Dr Kim Westerskov p. 5 (top), p. 13

All inquiries should be addressed to:
Barron's Educational Series, Inc.
250 Wireless Boulevard
Hauppauge, New York 11788
http://www.barronseduc.com

Library of Congress Catalog Card No. 00-041409
International Standard Book No. 0-7641-1599-5

Library of Congress Cataloging-in-Publication Data
Dunbier, Sally.
    Sea turtles / Sally Dunbier. – 1st ed, for the U.S. and Canada.
    p. cm – (Animals of the oceans)
    ISBN 0-7641-1599-5
    1. Sea turtles. I. Title. II. Series.

QL666.C536 D85 2000
597.92'8—dc21   00-041409

Printed in Hong Kong
9 8 7 6 5 4 3 2 1